Adriaen Block and the *Onrust*
Setting the Stage for Dutch Colonization of North America

Don Rittner

Dedication

To Adriaen Block and his crew of the *Onrust*

"Niemand kan regter zijn in zijne eigen zaken"

Copyright © 2016 by Don Rittner
First Printing in 2016

ISBN-10:0962426318
ISBN-13:978-0-9624263-1-5

Contact: drittner@aol.com

Table of Contents

Acknowledgements — i

Introduction — 1

17th Century Dutch Building Techniques on the Onrust — 2

Fire Bending — 8

Captain Adriaen Block — 13

Building the Onrust — 19

Block's Timeline — 37

Bibliography — 39

Acknowledgements

The author wishes to thank the following: Justyna Kostek, Herbert van Hasselt, Marieke Leeverink, Gemeente Amsterdam Stadsarchief, John Wolcott, National Archives of the Netherlands, and the Library of Congress.

Adriaen Block and the *Onrust*: Setting the Stage for Dutch Colonization of North America

Introduction

The importance of the Dutch occupation of North America and their contributions to American history in the 17th century hardly gets notice in most American schools. Henry Hudson, sailing for the Dutch, gets credit for discovering the river and valley that bears his name today although the Native population that lived there probably laughed at the thought. Textbooks are full of stories of the English based Pilgrims, the Virginia colonies, and even French explorations in Canada and the northern U.S. Often the Dutch are mentioned in passing with stories about Peter Stuyvesant having a wooden leg and Peter Minuit buying Manhattan for twenty four dollars. With the translation of thousands of Dutch colonial documents in recent years and publications such as Russell Shorto's *The Island at the Center of the World: The Epic Story of Dutch Manhattan and the Forgotten Colony That Shaped America* (Vintage Press, 2005), the importance of the Dutch contribution to American history is finally gaining some momentum.

One of the most important early Dutch explorers of the 17th century was Adriaen Block, a mariner and trader who successfully explored much of the Northeast United States and laid the groundwork for the Dutch colonization of much of the area that now comprises six northeastern states (New York, New Jersey, Pennsylvania, Maryland, Connecticut and Delaware) and in which he named New Netherland. He is usually mentioned in a sentence or two about building the first fur trading ship in America, named the *Onrust*, after his ship the *Tiger* burned somewhere in New York Bay in the winter of 1613.

Block's contribution was much more than simply building a ship. He created an extensive trade network during several expeditions with the indigenous populations in the Hudson Valley and beyond. He created the first map of the region which not only was a geographical guide but also an anthropological representation of the native populations then in existence.

Block's 1614 manuscript map surveys the North American Coast from Marblehead Bay, north of Cape Cod, to the Hudson River (The Noort Rivier or North River). He was the first European to navigate through the treacherous Hellegat, now the East River, and explore the harbors of Long Island and Connecticut, and circumnavigate Manhattan and Long Island. He identified the Housatonic and Thames Rivers and sailed up the Connecticut River (the Versche Rivier or Fresh River) all the way up to present day city of Hartford. "Adriaen Block Eylandt" (today Block Island) is named after the Dutch explorer. His map formed the basis for the New Netherland claim.

His most important contribution was ordering the building of the first permanent settlement of the Dutch in North America that began as a fur trading fort and eventually became the city of Albany, New York. This book adds knowledge about Block the man and his struggles building the *Onrust*.

17th Century Dutch Building Techniques on the *Onrust*

Every 17th century Dutch shipwright knew how to build their boats and saw little need to write those techniques down. No blueprints needed, just mental knowhow. When a shipwright died, the knowledge went with him or hopefully was passed onto a son. While that was sufficient 400 years ago, it poses a real problem for modern historians and maritime archeologists who want to know how the Dutch built their ships that were cheaper and faster than any other European nation during the early 17th century.

Shell First or Northern method shown here on a copper engraving by Sieuwert van der Meulen. Source: (naar) Sieuwert van der Meulen - Kopergravure 1700-1725. *Afbeelding van het bouwen van een schip*. You can see the wooden cleats and planking tongs (clamps) used to hold the planks together.

The Dutch were able to build ships cheaper and quicker and Dutch shipwrights were highly regarded though their "unscientific" methods were not. During the early 17th century the Netherlands, with only a million and a half inhabitants, had a fleet of almost 2000 cargo ships and that was more than France, England and Scandinavian countries combined.

In 1603, Sir Walter Raleigh complained in his "Observations Concerning the Trade and Commerce of English with the Dutch and other Foreign Nations,"

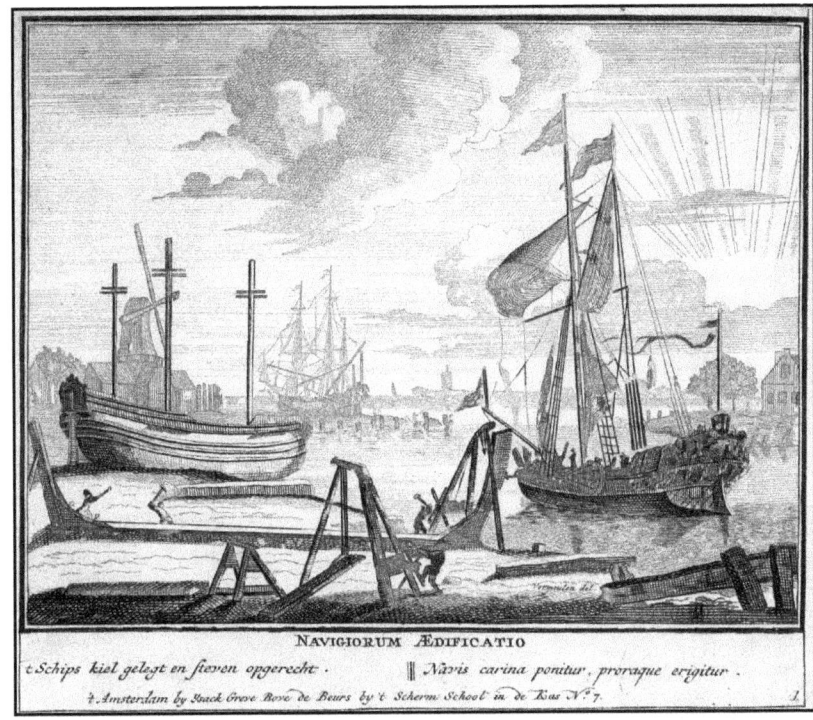

Copper engraving by Sieuwert van der Meulen showing the construction of a ship (1700-1725). Notice the stem and stern are erected and the device in the foreground to lift planks. Source: (naar) Sieuwert van der Meulen - Kopergravure 1700-1725. *Afbeelding van het bouwen van een schip.*

Nicolaas Witsen (1674-1717) by Petrus Schenk, 1701.

"...that the Dutch were everywhere outstripping the English, and especially monopolizing the carrying trade by the structure and roominess of their shipping holding much merchandise, though sailing with fewer hands than our ships could, thereby carrying their goods much cheaper to and from foreign parts that England can; whereby the Dutch gain all the foreign freight, whilst our ships lie idle and decay, or else go to Newcastle for coals." [1]

In the 1660s the French Finance Minister Jean-Baptiste Colbert ordered a number of Dutch ships be built and hired several Dutch shipwrights, including master-shipwright Jan Groen from Amsterdam in an effort to modernise the French shipbuilding industry. [2]

Peter the Great, the Tsar of Russia, wanted to build a navy but instead of hiring Dutch shipwrights, he

---

[1] Cawston, G., & Keane, A. H. (1968). The early chartered companies, A.D. 1296-1858. New York: B. Franklin. Pg. 43.

[2] Peters, A. (2013). Ship decoration 1630-1780. Barnsley: Seaforth Publishing. Pg. 122.

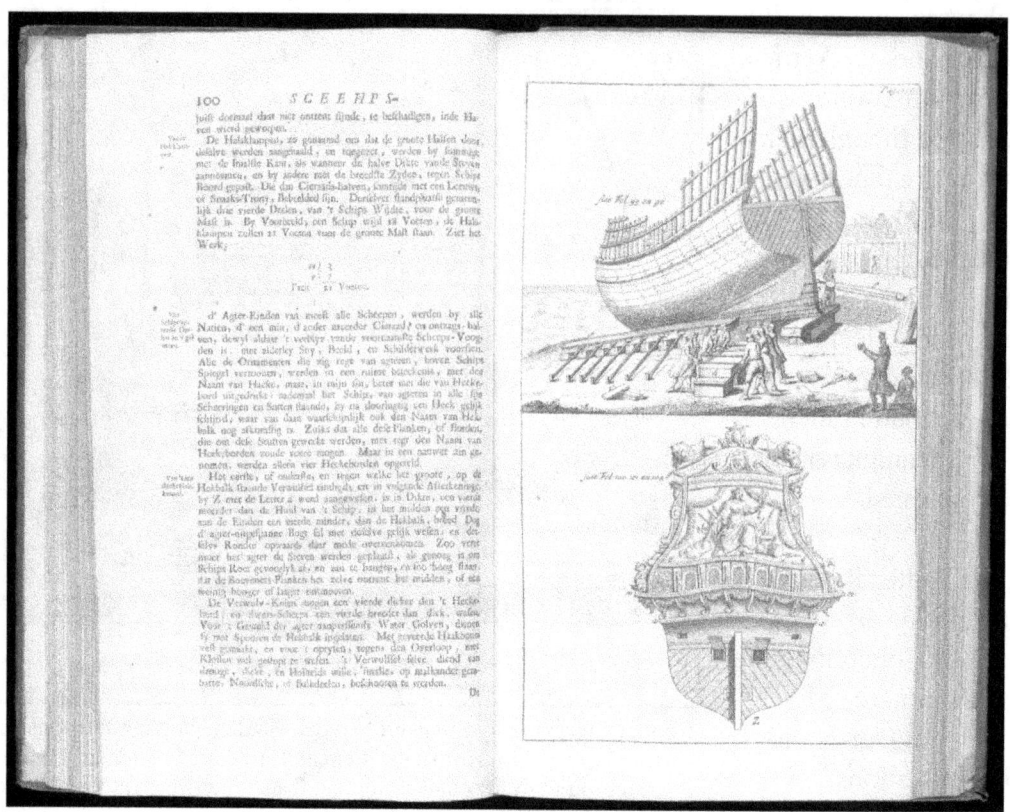

"Frame First" method as illustrated in Van Yk's *De Nederlandsche scheepsbouwkunst open Gestelt* (Dutch Naval Architecture Unveiled), 1697.

decided to go to the small village of Zaandam (Saardam) in 1697 where he signed up, disguised as a common sailor, to learn Dutch shipbuilding at the shipyards of Mynheer Calf. Under the alias of Peter Baas, he watched the shipbuilders closely, visited the small shops of sail makers and rope makers, but then went to Amsterdam after the villagers learned his identity and followed him everywhere like a rock star. He spent four months working the dockyards of the East India Company. When he finished working on the ship there the city of Amsterdam gave it to him as a present and he named it the *Amsterdam*.

However the Tsar did not like the rule of thumb method the Dutch used so he was unable to codify the building techniques of the Dutch for use back in Russia. He went off to England at their request and promise of a more scientific method. He was later quoted about the Dutch technique, stating, *"this art was not taught in the mathematical way, but only some principles of it, so that the rest must be acquired by long practice and experience."*[3] In the end Peter the Great hired Dutch ship builders. He probably reasoned maybe the Dutch were unscientific, but they built reliable and strong ships in a short time period.

---

[3] Cross, A. G. (2000). Peter the Great through British eyes: Perceptions and representations of the Tsar since 1698. Cambridge: Cambridge University Press. Pg. 14.

It also reasoned that to build a good Dutch boat you had to be in fact Dutch with the magic touch as Nicolaes Witsen alludes to in his shipbuilding treatment:

"It is surprising that foreigners, though they have studied economical building in the dockyards of this country, can never practice it in their own land… And this in my opinion proceeds from the fact that they are then working in an alien environment and with alien artisans. From which it follows that even if a foreigner had all the building rules in his head, they would not serve him, unless he had learned everything here in this country by experience, and still that would not help him, unless he should find a way to inculcate in his workmen the thrifty and neat disposition of the Hollander, which is impossible."

The use of oak in the Netherlands was important in shipbuilding. While the Dutch spent a great deal of time using high quality timber, they were not unwilling to use pine in places and wood that had a lot of sapwood in it to keep the costs and production time down – the average life of a Dutch boat was only 20 years. [4]

Also the use of outfitting windmills as saw mills beginning in 1592 created a way to produce consistently sized planks and lots of them. The first known sawmill was the mill called *Het Juffertje* that has been translated by different sources as "The Damsel" or "The Missy" and invented by Cornelis Corneliszoon of Uitgeest who obtained a patent on it in 1593 from the States of Holland. Juffertje is also a Dutch boy's name today and means dragonfly.[5] A 1798 Dutch dictionary defines Juffertje as "young lady, miss, girl, jgar, beam,

Allegory for the invention of the saw-mill, by Cornelis van Uitgeest, ca.1713-1752. North Holland Archives.

---

[4] Hoving, A. J., Wildeman, D., & Witsen, N. (2012). *Nicolaes Witsen and shipbuilding in the Dutch Golden Age.* College Station: Texas A & M University Press. Pg. 23

[5] Hills, R. L. (1994). *Power from wind: A history of windmill technology.* Cambridge: Cambridge University Press. Pgs. 166-167.

joint, and warming pan."[6] Another dictionary lists it as "a Little or young Gentlewoman." In a French dictionary damsel or Donielle in French and jeffertje in Dutch is listed as a damsel, or young gentlewoman.

By 1630 there were 83 sawmills north of Amsterdam and 52 of them were located in the Zaan district. This standardization and the use of pre-made frame parts were practical and efficient. The Netherlands received much of their lumber from the Baltic's and in fact during the 17th century it was the Dutch trading ships that moved most of the timber from this area to the European region. [7]

White oak has special properties that make it ideal for shipbuilding. It is one of the most water resistant and rot resistant trees. Part of the reason for that is in the cellular structure.

Parenchyma cells in the xylem, which is the tissue that is used for water and mineral transport in the tree, have special balloon like outgrowths on them known as tylosis.[8] They dam up the vascular tissue preventing water from seeping in. Also it prevents decay in the heartwood. Tylosis has been known since 1675 when Italian doctor and biologist Marcello Malpighi drew them in a cross section of chestnut.

Oaks that have tylosis in a consistent fashion are American White Oak, Blackjack, Garry, Overcup, Valley, Burr, Cow, Post and Swamp White Oaks. European oak (Quercus petraea/sessiliflora, Quercus robur/pendunculata), oak that Block would have been familiar with in Europe is similar to American White Oak except it is practically sap free.

Black Locust also has tylosis along with Large Tooth Aspen, Hardy Catalpa, Desert Willow, Shellbark, Bitternut, Nutmeg and Shagbark Hickories, Butternut, Black Walnut, Red Mulberry and Orange Osage.

Other species that have some tylosis are Black Oak, Yellow Buckeye, Beech, Red Gum (sap), Yellow Poplar, Magnolias, Sycamore, Black Cottonwood, Eucalyptus (blue gum), White and Oregon Ashes, and the Elms.

Species that have no tylosis are Maples, Birches, Blue Beech, Flowering Dogwood, Holly, Silver

---

[6] Sewel, W. (1766). A complete dictionary, English and Dutch, to which is added a grammar, for both languages. Amsterdam: Kornelis de Veer. Pg. 122.

[7] Jouko Tossevainen,. Dutch Forests Products' trade in the Baltic from the Late Middle Ages to the Pece of Munster in 1648. 149 pp.; Barbour, Violet. 1930. Dutch and English Merchant Shipping in the Seventeenth Century. Masters Thesis. Pp. 261-290.

[8] Zimmermann, M. H. (1983). Xylem structure and the ascent of sap. Berlin: Springer-Verlag. Pps 232-237; Kishima, T. (1966). Review of tylosis formation in hardwood vessels. Washington, D.C.: U.S. Dept. of Agriculture, Forest Service. 10 pps.

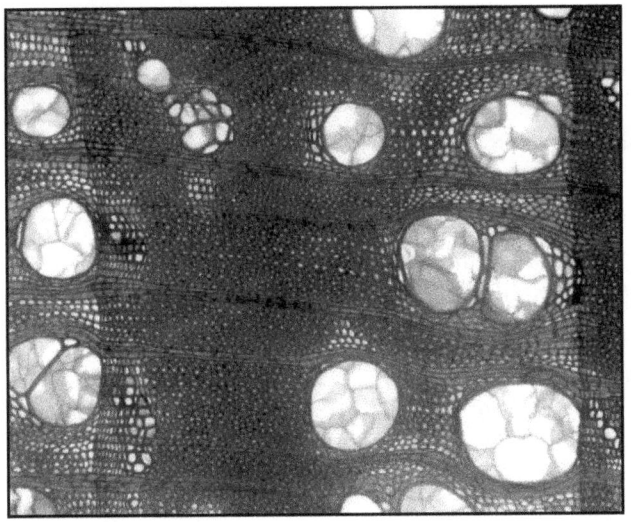

Tyloses are small bladder like extensions that prevent water from entering the vascular system of certain trees like White Oak and as seen here Black Locust making them ideal for ship building. In this microphotograph 20x magnification you can see the tyloses completely filling the vessels preventing water from seeping in. Photo courtesy of James Mauseth, The University of Texas.

Bell, Black and Water Gums, Back and Red Cherry, Basswood, Persimmon, and Honey Locust.

Some pines have a scattering of tylosis in them.

In one study, 139 tree species were examined for tylosis and 56 species belonging to 25 genera contained them.

The other ability of white oak is the fact that when heated the cellular structure becomes pliable, and when heated the wood can be bent and twisted to form the desirable shape, like fitting a plank to the futtocks. When the oak cools it retains those shapes. This is due to polymers in the wood called hemicelluloses. They are resin like and when heated they soften making the wood pliable.[9]

The early 17th century Dutch shipwright did not know the scientific reason for the oaks being the best wood for shipbuilding. They simply knew these characteristics existed. Or as Witsen stated:

"For Shipbuilding, oak tops everything, above all over trees, because it is tough, bends well, is strong and not too heavy."[10]

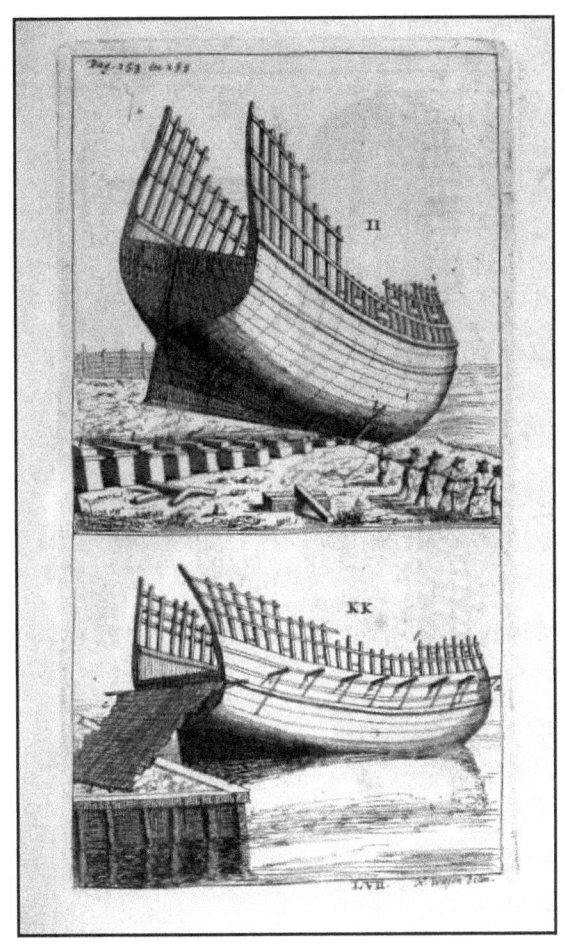

Witsen illustration showing how a ship is finished by putting into water after it's built to the water line.

---

[9] Gerry, E. (1914). Tyloses: Their occurrence and practical significance in some American woods. Washington, D.C.: Dept. of Agriculture. Pg. 445-470 plus plates.

[10] Hoving, pg. 24.

Fire Bending

One of the most fascinating aspects of early Dutch ship building is fire bending. The successful use of fire to bend the planks so they fit the hull snugly is an art form rarely used today.

The use of fire by humans for things other than cooking has been known for centuries. In North America, lawyer and sheriff for New Netherland Adrian Van der Donck talked about the use of fire by Native Americans in his 'Description of New Netherland," published in 1655.

"The Indians are in the habit- and we Christians have also adopted it - once a year in the fall to burn the woods, plains and those marshlands that are not too wet, as soon as the leaves have dropped and the herbage has withered. Portions that were missed out, as may happen, get their turn later in the months of March or April. This is known among our people as well as the Indians there as bush burning, and is practiced for several reasons, some of which we shall briefly note.

For one, it facilitates hunting, because the dry weeds and fallen leaves not only hinder the hunter's progress, but the crackling invariably betrays him, and the game spots him first. Second, it serves to thin out the forest as the fire smothers and kills much new undergrowth. Third, it clears the forest of old deadwood consisting of branches and fallen trees; and fourth, it raises the game and assists the hunter since it restricts the animals' movements and also enables them to be traced in the burned areas.

Bush burning is an extraordinary and spectacular event. Seen from a distance it would seem that not only the leaves, weeds, and deadwood are being consumed, but that all the trees and the whole of the surrounding forest are falling prey to the flames. Fall being a dry season over there, the fire burns fiercely and spreads fast so that it is terrifying to watch. When the fire rages near houses, homesteads, and wooden fencing one has to be careful lest he suffer damage, as happened at first before people watched out for it, when several houses burned down. Green trees are not at risk, however; the outer bark is charred for a foot or two from the ground, but it does not kill them.

In very dense stands of pine trees that are old and resinous it happens that the fire sweeps upwards, because dying trees have fallen against and across each other or remained halfway standing and dried out. In those trees the fire settles and spreads upwards along them, and when it reaches the gluey, resinous branches /17/ and knots, it begins to blaze fiercely and flies from tree to tree, so that sometimes a good part of the top only is burned away, or the entire tree may fall down. A whole lot of trees are thus destroyed, but it never happens that all of the bush-burns down. I have seen many instances of it in the Colony of Rensselaerswyck, which has much pinewood. Such a fire is a splendid sight when one sails on the rivers at night while the forest is ablaze on both banks. Fire and flames are seen everywhere and on all sides.

Much of the blaze is driven on by the wind and follows what it feeds on, but in many spots dry wood and dead trees keep on burning; it is a delightful scene to look on from afar." [11]

Walter Raleigh wrote about the Indians in Virginia using fire to fell trees and make dug out canoes using resin laid on the parts to be excavated and then burned. They would scoop out the burned areas to make the log hollow.

A very good description of the fire process was written by Swedish Botanist Peter Kalm. He wrote about the use of fire by Native Americans to create dugout canoes on the Delaware River

---

[11] Adriaen Van der Donck,. Description of New Netherland. 1655. Pps 21-22.

in 1747. The process was the same as written by Raleigh except the natives used twigs instead of resin. He wrote:

"When the Indian intend to fell a tree, for want of proper instruments they employ fire; they set fire to a quantity of wood at the roots of the tree, and in order that the fire might not reach further up than they would have it, they fasten some rags to a pole, dip them in water, and keep continually washing the tree a little above the fire until the lower part is burnt nearly through; it is then pulled down. When they intend to hollow a tree for a canoe, they lay dry branches along the stem of the tree as far as it must be hollowed out, set them on ire, and replace them by others. While these parts are burning, they keep pouring water on those parts that are not to be burnt at the sides and ends. When the interior is sufficiently burnt out, they take their stone hatchets and shells and scoop out the burnt wood. These canoes are usually thirty or forty feet long."[12]

It has already been discussed the unique characteristics in white oak that allow it to become rot and water-resistant. The ability to become pliable when heated and retain shapes is probably the most important characteristic of the tree.

In 1590, Flemish printer Theodore de Bry published a series of John White illustrations of natives in Virginia (actually North Carolina). This one depicts canoe making using fire.

---

[12] Kalm, P. (1771). Travels into North America: Containing its natural history, and a circumstantial account of its plantations and agriculture in general. London: Editor. English Translation by John Reinhold Forster. Vol. II. Pp 37-40.

Obviously there are very few straight lines on the hull of a ship. The frames, which form the skeleton, are bent and the planks that fit the frames are the skin on the skeleton and need to conform to the overall shape of the skeleton. During the 17th century one man could use fire to bend a plank although two were often used for bends and twists. During Witsen's time planks were heated over an iron bar hanging on two sawhorses with a fire created by burning straw. Another method was a fire pit dug in the ground and by using one or two wooden sawhorses placed on the opposite sides of the fire, the fire bender would place the plank on the sawhorse and a large boulder on the end of the plank. As the wood softened the weight of the boulder would bend the plank. By hand, he would have to twist the plank to get the angles he needed. The fire bender would constantly brush some water on the plank as it was heating to prevent cracking and catching on fire.

Later during the early 18th century an English Captain named Cumberland invented a stove where planks would be laid in sand, moistened with water, above the fire, and after hot enough taken out and bent. The description sounds too cumbersome but the description goes on to say:

"This method excels that of burning the Planks over an open Fire in feveral refpects: particularly, that no part of the Wood is deftroy'd, but remains of the fame Dimenfions; at leaft very nearly; a Plank of the breadth of 16 inches being faid not to alter above 1/20 part of an Inch. The Edges of the Plank are preferv'd; and confequently the Work muft be much firmer, and the Calking laft longer. The extraordinary foftnefs of the Wood, while 'tis warm, makes it eafily bend to any Figure neceffary in Ship-building, which it holds very well, if they have occafion to take it off again after it is cold – whereas the Plank bent by burning, would ftart when loofened; and could be fixed to the Timbers by fuch a force, as was able to overcome the Refiftance occafion'd by the Spring of the Plank. It likewife adapts it felf very readily to the Surface of the Timbers, if they happen to be uneven."[13]

The report goes on to say that it takes five or six hours to make a plank ready for bending. Certainly not the Dutch method.

The surviving main documentation on 17th century Dutch ship building comes from two sources: Nicolaes Witsen and his *Aeloude en Hedendaegsche Scheepsbouw en Bestier* (Ancient and Modern Shipbuilding and Management) in 1671 and Cornelis Van Yk and his *De Nederlandsche scheepsbouwkunst Open Gestelt* (Dutch Naval Architecture Unveiled) published in 1697. Witsen and Van Yk had different viewpoints on how to construct ships, but that was due to their different locations in the Netherlands and indeed there were two different shipbuilding traditions being played out. While the initial stages of laying the keel, raising the stem and sternposts, and adding the first set of planks (called strakes) on both sides of the keel up to the water line were identical; the methods went in different directions after that.

These two men were not the only ones writing about shipbuilding, however. Other shipbuilding books were written by authors that described the English, Spanish, Portuguese, French, German

---

[13]Gray, J., Reid, A., Innys, W., & Manby, R. (1733). The philosophical transactions (from the year 1720, to the year 1732) abridged, and disposed under general heads. London: Printed for William Innys and Richard Manby, printers to the Royal Society, at the West End of St. Paul's. Pg. 400.

and Swedish methods. Many can be found on the Internet in digital form, but Witsen and Van Yk are the principal techniques likely used for building the *Onrust*.

In 17th century Netherlands these two schools of shipbuilding methods were in vogue simultaneously, although one was older. Witsen describes the "Shell or Planks First" system, also known as the Northern Method, while Van Yk describes the "Frame or Skeleton First" System, also known as the Southern Method, similar to those used today. The "Shell First" system is older, traced back before the Middle Ages, and was the system used in constructing the *Onrust*.

Witsen describes a system where the shell of the ship is first built up to the bilge area where it starts to turn and then planking of the hull occurs. Frames are then fitted into the "shell" formed by the outside planking. The first set of planks are held together with small wooden cleats and planking tongs. The floor timbers and futtocks are then inserted and framed.

Van Yk's techniques are similar to modern methods where the planks are affixed to preexisting frames; that is, the frames are erected first and then the skin or planking is completed.

> Shell or Planks First System = Northern Method = Witsen
> Frame or Skeleton First System = Southern Method = Van Yk

The planks abut each other and the technique is known as carvel planking. The method is named for its first use on building the caravel, also known as karvelle or karveel, a Portuguese ship type. By the 15th century, carvel became known as both a ship and a type of hull construction.

Both the Northern and Southern Methods of shipbuilding occurred during the 17th century and in different regions of the Netherlands, but it was the "Skeleton First" method that eventually became the most widely used, after nearly 2,000 years of using the "Shell First" system. Witsen was familiar with shipbuilding techniques in the region known as Zaan Kant (Zaan River in Amsterdam) while Van Yk was familiar with building techniques centered in "de Maze" (Meuse or Maas River, the city of Rotterdam and further south). Both regions were separated only by little more than sixty miles.

It appears that in some cases, both methods were employed building the same ship, starting with the "Shell First" method up to the water line. Then the "Frame First" method is used after that, or in various combinations.

Nicolaes Corneliszoon Witsen was born on May 8, 1641 and was a lawyer and burgomaster of Amsterdam. Witsen was also a cartographer, artist, expert on Russia, and lover of science. He died in 1717. Witsen was not a shipbuilder. Van Yk was a retired shipwright when he wrote his book on the subject and is considered a better source than Witsen on the issue by some, but not all, ship historians. For example, noted ship historian A. J. Hoving explains that Witsen goes into much more detail than the experienced shipwright Van Yk although Witsen never built a boat. Witsen published two editions of his tome in 1671 and 1690. Only five copies of the second edition exist. Unfortunately, his shipbuilding book was not very well organized and was confusing to many researchers. To make matters worse, Witsen and Van Yk had different names for the same parts. Witsen called floor timbers *buikstuk* but Van Yk called them *leggers* or *vloerwrangen*. In addition, Witsen's descriptions are for building a *pinas* not a yacht per se, the class of ship the Onrust belongs to, although the basic instructions are the same for the early construction phase. A *pinas* is a heavily built *fluyt* with a deeper draught, according to ship historian Richard Unger. By the later 17th century, pinas and yachts were more or less synonymous, according to Hoving.

Over the last few years, Witsen's work has been analyzed and presented in a more easily understood format specifically by researchers like Hoving. Many items combined to contribute to the rediscovery of 17th century Dutch shipbuilding: the interpretation of Witsen's writings; archeological evidence derived from excavating and retrieving shipwrecks from the reclaimed Zuiderzee (a former inland sea) while reverse engineering their construction; the study of early 17th century paintings (iconography); *bestekkens* (contract specifications); *certers* (shipwright's notes); and *charters* (used by large companies like the Dutch East India Company for specific classes of ships).

The original *Onrust* was a sprit-rigged leeboard yacht. Yacht, or to be more accurate, *jacht*, *jagt* or *jaghen* is the Dutch spelling, meaning "to hunt, or hunting, or chase." *Ter jagt gaan* is translated as "to go a hunting." Early yachts were loaded with cannons and used by the Dutch sailors and soldiers when the Dutch were fighting for their independence. Yachts, because of their quick maneuverability (hydrodynamics), were used to chase down enemy ships and blow them out of the water.

By the later 17th century, a 1675 English dictionary defines yacht as "a small ship or pleasure boat," or in Dutch "zeyljagt" or "zeiljacht" translates to a sailing pleasure boat.

The modern use of the word yacht, or the impression that they were more than pleasure boats, has to be blamed on England's Charles II. Upon his restoration to the crown in 1660 - he was exiled to the Netherlands - he rode aboard a yacht from Breda to Rotterdam once owned by the Prince of Orange. He fell in love with the yacht and when he expressed his admiration for it, Van Vlooswick, Burgomaster of Amsterdam and the States General of the Netherlands presented him with his own yacht and just as elegant. He named it *Mary* after his sister. He was also given many paintings sculptures and furniture plus the yacht that was known as the "Dutch Gift" of 1660 to foster good relations between the two countries.

Charles and his brother James, Duke of York, then began the sport of yacht racing – they had the first race on October 1, 1661. Only four years later the Dutch and English were at war again in the Second Anglo-Dutch War of 1665-67. So much for gifts!

The original *Mary* - England's first yacht - sunk on March 25, 1675 as the yacht struck a rock and 35 people on board, including the Earl of Meath, died. *Mary* was rediscovered and excavated by amateur divers in 1971 seven miles from Holyhead, Anglesey in the United Kingdom almost directly across from Dublin in the Irish Sea.

Captain Adriaen Block

Our story of the *Onrust* begins with its Captain Adriaen Courtsen Block who was born around 1567 in Amsterdam and was the son of Court Block. Originally he lived on the water on the Damrak, a partially filled canal in the center of Amsterdam between present day Amsterdam Central Railway Station and Dam Square, running north south.

We do not know much about Block's childhood but we do know that Block was always a captain or skipper during his adult life. Thanks to research conducted and published by Simon Hart[14] and Isaac Newton Phelps Stokes[15] in the mid 20th century, we do know some of Block's history.

Block owned a ship called the *Liefde* (Love) that weighed 350 tons and in April 1596, he sailed to Langesund in Norway to obtain a cargo of wood. While in Norway, in order to purchase this wood, Block obtained a guarantee or "loan" from his charterer, Coenraat van Sweeden, worth 600 guilders on bottomry. "Bottomry" is when a captain borrows money against the bottom or keel of his ship, basically insuring that the person who loaned the money will get the ship if the borrower defaults - a 17th century form of liability insurance. This practice was well known as far back as ancient Grecian era; a nice arrangement, although in principle the repayment would be contingent on the ship completing the voyage and the loan paid with considerable interest, but if the ship was lost the loan was forgiven.

Block then sailed north of England to Bilbao, Spain and emptied the ship. He received another commission from Bilbao to go to Ribadeo, Spain where he picked up more wood and took it to Cadiz in southwestern Spain.

On April 23, 1601, Block sailed with 13 other ships to the East Indies as captain of the *Zwarte Leeuw* (Black Lion). This was part of the famous Admiral Jacob van Heemskerk's fleet and Block captained Vice Admiral Jean Grenier's ship. Block returned with the ship in 1603 and that year - now at the age of 36 - he married Neeltgen (or Neeltje) Heyndricx (or Heinrix) van Gelder on October 26 in Amsterdam. She was born around 1581; her age was about 22 when she married Adriaen. They had five children, a daughter Stijntje (Stijntjen) who was born in 1604 (baptized December 27, 1607); a son Court was born in 1608 (died young, after 1627); twins, a daughter Neeitje, born in 1615 (baptized on July 21, 1615 and also died young, sometime after 1627); a son Jan, born in 1615 (also baptized on July 21, 1615), and the youngest daughter

---

[14]Hart, S. (1959). The prehistory of the New Netherland Company: Amsterdam notarial records of the first Dutch voyages to the Hudson. Amsterdam: City of Amsterdam Press. 105 pp.

[15]Stokes, I. N., Wieder, F. C., Paltsits, V. H., & Smith, S. L. (1915). The iconography of Manhattan island, 1498-1909. New York: R.H. Dodd.

Greitje who was born in 1617.

Another source lists two Neeltje Block's with baptism dates of October 23, 1612 and July 21, 1615 and a son Henrik baptized on June 20, 1610. It is not confirmed that Henrik or the Neeltje of October 23rd were children of our Block.

Block's house at 34 Oude Waal Street is still standing. Photo by Marieke Leeverink.

Not to be further confused with our Adriaen Block, there was four other Adriaen Blocks living in the region around the same time. Adriaen Jacobsz Block (1565-1606)[16] was a cloth dealer who lived on the Nieuwendijk in Amsterdam; Adriaen Martensz Block (1582-1661)[17], a merchant in Amsterdam; Adriaen Rutgers Block (1560 or 1561-1630),[18] and Adriaen Willemsz Block[19] who died in 1626 in Gravenmoer (Noord-Brabant).

Dutch history records indicate that the other "Adriaens" were not the captain Adriaen Block: Adriaen Jacobsz Block married Catharina van Essen and had a daughter Lysbeth Block (1589?-1655). Adriaen Martensz Block married Catharina Gerards Van Der Laen and had two daughters Adriana and Catharina, both born about 1610. Adriaen Rutgers Block married Anneke Rutgers and had one child Engelken Arlensdr Block (married Peter de Groot) (1600-1645). We

---

[16]http://www.genealogieonline.nl/stamboom-familie-baijens/I574.php; http://terlouw.voorouders.net/person/13/i_I7198/adriaen-jacobsz-block

[17]http://www.genealogieonline.nl/en/stamboom-baris/I64282.php; Brial, Pierre. 2001a. Le retlationd'Adriaen Martensz Block. Bull. Soc. George. Reunion 1:3-4.

[18]http://www.geni.com/people/Adriaen-Rutgers-Block/6000000002301670077; http://www.genealogieonline.nl/en/stamboom-baris/I53550.php

[19]http://www.genealogieonline.nl/en/stamboom-karels-hulsbos/I4809.php

Reinier Nooms (1623-64) printmaker produced this illustration of the Montelbaanstoren on the Oudeschans in 1678. Block's house would be a few houses down the canal on the left obscured from view from all the boats in the canal. Courtesy of Gemeente Amsterdam Stadsarchief.

know nothing about Adriaen Williemsz Block other than he had a son Steven Adriaense Block, who was born around 1595 and died in 1657.[20]

Our Adriaen Block's daughter Stijntje married skipper Jacob Lambrechts on September 4, 1639. Their son Jan was third mate of the *Walvisch* and sailed to the East Indies in October 1649. Another daughter, Grietje, married Jacob Jansz Roehof.[21]

In the spring of 1604, Block sailed from the Goereese Gat, between the delta islands of Goeree and Voorn in South Holland to Leghorn, Italy on the 400 ton *Grote Roode Leeuw* (Great Red Lion). He unloaded his cargo, took his payment to Cyprus and purchased a cargo of *"cotton, rice (1828 bales), gall-nuts (100 bags), currants and malmsey* (a wine grape)." With that cargo he sailed to Venice, however he was not able to sell the ship or cargo so set sail to go back to Amsterdam.

Just off Lisbon, he captured a ship from Lubeck belonging to Hans Maes that was full of sugar and Brazilian wood. The ship was going to Lisbon from Pernambuco and Block had a "Letter of Marque" allowing him to capture any enemy ship. A "Letter of Marque and Reprisal" is a letter or approval from the government allowing a person, known as a privateer, to attack and capture

---

[20]http://www.genealogieonline.nl/en/stamboom-karels-hulsbos/I4809.php

[21]Hart. Page 48.

Closeup of Block's house at 34 Oude Waal Street. Photo by Justyna Kostek.

Block had a good view of the Montelbaen Tower from his house (on right). Photo by Justyna Kostek.

enemy vessels and their cargo – basically a government sanctioned pirate. The captured ship would be brought back and the admiralty courts would sell the property.

Block arrived back in Amsterdam in August 1605 with the captured ship and cargo that was appraised at 180,000 guilders in which Block shared the profits. The ship and free merchandise was returned to Maes but the rest of the cargo sold. With his profits, Block now bought a house called "De Twee Bontecraijen" (The Two Hooded Crows) at 34 Oude Waal Street near the Montelbaanstoren, a tower on the bank of the canal Oudeschans. The original tower was built in 1516 as a defensive position but was rounded to its present form in 1606, the year Adriaen moved there. He lived in this house his whole adult life. The house still survives. Oude Waal means old haven surrounded by piers for ships.

Not everything was rosy for Block, however, at this time. Block owned one-sixteenth share in the company that had sent out the ship, the *Great Red Lion*. The other owners, along with Adriaen Block and his 1/16th share, were Pieter Gerritsz. van? Ruytenburch 1/8 share; Hans van den Eijnde 1/16; Bernart Berrewijns 1/16 [he also owned the Witte Leeuw (White Lion)]; Cornelia Snellincx 1/16; Jorgen Timerman 1/32; Symon Willemsz Nooms 1/16; Jan de Barlaimont 1/16; Pieter Rousseau 1/16; Abraham van Lemens 1/18; and the Rotterdam merchants Johan van der Veken and Pieter Lenertsz. Busch.

Jan and Jacomo van Lemens, who were factors (agents) in Block's company in Venice, went bankrupt and therefore payments were held up. Block and his partners, in turn, sued their fellow owner Abraham van Lemens over it. As a result in August of 1607, Block sold the *Groote Roode Leeuw* for 18,000 guilders representing all his partners.[22]

It appears that Block's first excursion to North America was in May, 1611 as a "Supercargo" along with Hendrick Christiaensen serving the same function onboard the *St. Pieter* that was captained by Cornelis Rijser. The excursion was chartered by Arnout Vogels and two merchant brothers, Leonard and Francoys Pelgrom of the Van Tweenhuysen Company. A supercargo is the person in charge of buying and selling the merchandise on a ship.

In 1612 Block purchased a boat, the square stern 100-ton *Fortuyn* from Olphert Pietersz. Schroor from Oostzaan for Block's employer, the Lambert Van Tweenhuysen Company. Francoys Pelgrom's nephew, Jan Kindt, was Block's Supercargo. He had a successful trade that year with the maiden voyage of the *Fortuyn*.

Block apparently knew Lambert van Tweenhuysen as early as 1606 when they both signed a lottery list [Lotteries were often held to help non profit organizations and particular in the arts]. Next to Block's signature was his motto: *"Every one seeks his own profit according to my opinion. In the earthly valley is small sorrow. If I draw a blank, inform me about it in Amsterdam."* Next to Van Tweenhuysen's signature was his motto: *"Who knows if it be true?"* Schroor's eagerness to sell the *Fortuyn* may have been that he needed to get out of town. He had just swindled his ship owners from deliveries that he was to have made to privateers in Mamora on the coast of Barbary in 1611. He also was charged with bringing a pardon to the privateers there from the States General.

It appears that Block made his second visit to America on the *Fortuyn* at the beginning of 1612 and a third voyage at the end of 1612. Each trip to what is now the Northeast coast of the United States, then called Nova Virginia, took about ten weeks to sail.

On one of the 1612 voyages occurred the first confrontation between Block and someone who would become his nemesis, Thijs Volckertsz. Mossel. On this particular visit, Mossel was offering the Native Americans double the offer Block made for their furs. The dispute lasted for months after they returned.

Block returned from the latter 1612 voyage at the end of July 1613. Christiaensen's role in this voyage is not clear; Jacob Eelkens or Eelckens, a Walloon from Rouen, is listed as Block's Supercargo. We do know that Eelkens served under Christiaensen in a later 1613 voyage and also temporarily served as commis of Fort Nassau when they built it in 1614, on Castle Island (present Albany, NY) with members of the *Fortuyn*.

---

[22]Hart. Pages 49-50.

During this earlier 1613 period Christiaensen and Eelkens supposedly signed a covenant with the Mohawk Indians in the Albany area known as the Treaty of Tawasantha (modern day Normanskill Valley, south of Albany) on April 21, 1613 on the hill known as Tawagonshi. The so-called treaty was brought to light in the 1950s by L. G. van Loon, a medical doctor and amateur historian. However, the document was later declared a forgery by Dutch scholars. If the treaty is authentic, it would be earliest known formal trade arrangement between Europeans and the Iroquois and a blueprint for those that followed.[23]

The Treaty of Tawasantha is not mentioned in Hart's *Prehistory*. However, it is obvious that some form of understanding or agreement must have been made with the indigenous populations that Block encountered in his several voyages. He produced a map of his voyages that depicted more than twenty Native nations that he either visited or was given information about. Some of the Natives listed on the Block and later Hendrickson Maps include:

Aquamachukes (*Atquanachuke*), Capitannasses (*Onondaga*), Gachoos (*Cayuga*), Iotecas (*Juniata*), Mahicans, Makimanes (*Mahican*), Manhattes, Maquaas (*Mohawk*), Mechkentiwoom (*Mechkentowoon*), Minquaas (*Conestoga, Iroquois*), Morhicans (*Mohegans*), Nahican (*Nahantics*), Nawaas, Pachami (*Nochpeem*), Pequats (*Pequots*), Sangicans (*Assumpink*), Sauwanew (*Shawnee*), Senecas, Sequins (*Mattabesec*), Stanckkans (*Assumpink*), Tappans, Wapanoos (*Wampanoag*), Waronawanka (*Waranawonkong*), Wikagykl (*Wecquaesgeek*), and Worenecks (*Waoranec*).

Block was given permission by the Native population in what is the present day New York City area to build the *Onrust* on land and was later given permission to build a fort by those Native landowners (Mohicans) in the area that is now Albany. Earlier when a Juan (Jan) Rondriquz was rescued by Christiaensen in the New York area, he had been trading for a year with the Natives so it seems obvious that relationships were made and continued.

After Block's return to Amsterdam, a letter dated July 30, 1613 was written by one of the men aboard the *Fortuyn,* Francoys Pelgroms Geerartsen to his wife:

"Further, dearest love, I cannot help telling you in this letter about the successful arrival of our ship under master Adriaen Block and our nephew Jan Kin for which God be praised. Both are in good health and made a good voyage, yes, a better voyage even that last year."[24]

He also wrote to his wife a month later on August 20, 1613 stating:

"...Further, dearest love, I could only find an opportunity to send you this short letter, for which I can hardly find any time, because I am so hard at work sending Adriaen Block out again to the same place

---

[23]Harjo, S. S. (n.d.). Nation to nation: Treaties between the United States & American Indian Nations. 272 pps.; Milholland, S. K. (2008). Native voices and native values in sacred landscapes management bridging the indigenous values gap on public lands through co-management policy. 255 pps.

[24]Hart, Notarial Records, p. 74.

from where he returned. We shall now send two ships thither and obtained a charter, so that no one but us is allowed to sail there. Will you please keep this a secret so that no one will know and hear about it?"[25]

Building the *Onrust*

Our story then begins with Block's fourth and final trip to the Northeast coast of North America in October 1613. This time Block was captain of the Tiger (*Tijger*), Hendrick Christiaensen was captain of the Fortune (*Fortuyn*) and a third ship, the Nightingale (*Nachtegael*), was captained by Mossel, Block's old nemesis.

Two other ships, the Little Fox (*het Vosken*, or the *Vos*) captained by Pieter Fransz, who was killed by the Natives and the ship later captained by Jan de With and another ship also called The Fortune (*de Fortuyn*) captained by Cornelis Jacobsz May, are part of the story too.

Adriaen Block and Hendrick Christiaensen may have been the first to sail to the territory that was to become New Netherland, to trade after Henry Hudson made his "discovery" of the river valley that bears his name. Nicolaes van Wassenaer in his *Historisch Verhael Aller Gedenckwaerdiger Geschiedenissen* (Historical Account of All the Most Remarkable Events which have happened in Europe, Etc.) published in 1625 writes:

"This country, or the River Montagne, called Mauritius by us, was first sailed to by the worthy Hendrick Christiaensz. of Cleves. After a voyage to the West Indies, he happened near there. But his vessel being laden and a ship belonging to Monickendam having been wrecked in that neighborhood, he durst not approach that land; this he postponed, being desirous to do so another time. It so happened that he and the worthy Adriaen Block chartered a ship, with the skipper Ryser, and accomplished a voyage thither, bringing back with him two sons of the principal sachem. Though very dull men, they were expert enough in knavery. Hudson, the famous English pilot had also been there, to reach the South Sea, but found no passage, as one may read in the Netherlands history, in the year 1612."[26]

Block had brought two Native American boys back to the Netherlands, Valentine and Orson, no doubt named after the early 13th century French story about two twin brothers abandoned in the woods.

Actually the Hudson had several names previously. The first use of the term "Hudson River" was recorded by the Dutch five years after Hudson "discovered" it, and not used until twelve years later by the English. The various names of the river and first record of it were:
Reviere van Nova Virginia (River of New Virginia), August 20, 1613
Reviere Montanges,' July 23, 1614; [Fr spelling is "Montagnes" and means "mountains"]
River of Montanea, July 23, 1614;

---

[25] Hart, Notarial Records, p. 74.

[26] Jameson, J. F. (1953). Narratives of New Netherland: 1609-1664. New York: Barnes & Noble. Nicolaes Van Waasenaer,. "Historicsch Verhael" in Narratives of New Netherland: 1609-1664. John Franklin Jameson. 1909. Applewood's American Philosophy and Religion Series. P. 78.

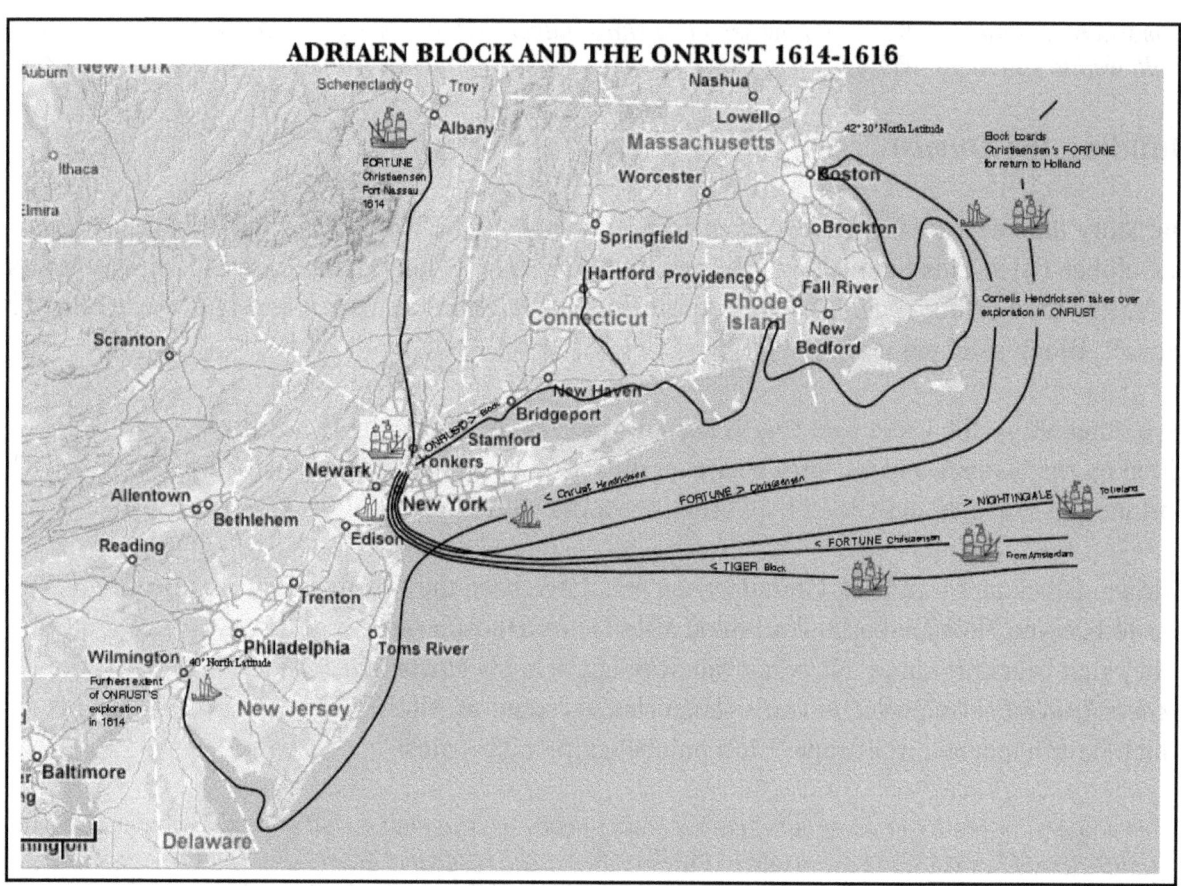

The route of the Onrust as it explored the East coast from 38 to 45 degrees north latitude. Map by Marieke Leeverink.

Riviere d'Hudson, August 13-14, 1614;
Riviere van der Vorst; Mauritius,' map of Adriaen Block 1614;
Rio de Montagna, Sept. 9, 1619;
Hudson River, 1621 (in English documents);
Rio de Montaigne, October 22, 1622;
Mauritius River, 1624;
The Noordrivier (North River), 1625;
Manhattes River, 1625;
Great River, 1630;
Nassau River, 1630.

The original inhabitants of the river in the Hudson-Mohawk Valleys, the Mohicans, called the river the *Mohicanittuck*, which means the *"river that flows both ways."*

There are records that state in 1598 that Dutch whalers were sent out by Gerrit Bicker and company and had been at the North (Hudson) and South (Delaware) Rivers that was recorded by the Directors of the Dutch West India Company in 1644. However, many scholars debunk this citing not enough primary evidence to prove it.

Block's Figurative Map of 1614 was instrumental in the formation of The New Netherland Company that had a three year privilege to carry on trade. Original in The Hague.

The voyages of these five ships, the Tiger, both Fortunes, Nightingale, and Little Fox, in late 1613 is where our story begins about The *Onrust*. All of the ships and crew were set out to explore the east coast, or the elusive Northwest Passage, locate Native American villages, create a trade network, or carry on trade. Each of them had their routes to follow. They did not leave together from the Netherlands nor did they all return together. Three ships: Block's Tiger (*Tijger*), Hendrick Christiaensen's Fortune (*Fortuyn*) and Mossel's Nightingale (*Nachtegael*) are the centerpieces of the Onrust's story.

In the fall of 1613 three ships representing two different companies were outfitted to sail to the New World, the *Fortuyn* under command of Hendrick Christiaensen; the *Tijger* under the captain of Adriaen Block; and the *Nachtegael* under the command of Thijs Mossel. Both the *Fortuyn* and *Tijger* were owned by the Van Tweenhuysen Company and the *Nachtegael* was owned by the Hans Claesz Company.

Block was, in fact, captain of both ships, the Tijger and Fortuyn, since he was in charge of the voyage's entire operation. Block's boss offered his competitors one-third of the trade with two-thirds going to Christiaensen and Block. Claesz Company did not agree and they warned Van Tweenhuysen that he would be held responsible if there was any trouble between the two competing groups in the same area. Van Tweenhuysen's company filed an affidavit asserting its rights to the fur trade. To be on the safe side, or for that matter winning side, Block asked to borrow some six or eight navy guns of 1500 to 1600 pounds each from the Amsterdam Admiralty in September 1613 for the *Tijger*, a request that was approved. He was loaned six guns. However, he had to put up a bail of 10 guilders per 100 pounds as a security deposit on the guns.

Christiaensen beat Mossel to the New York Bay and found a lone runaway, Juan Rodriguez, on the island. One source tells us Rodriguez had run away the year before, from the *Jonge Tobias* (Thijs Mossel was captain) and took with him guns, swords, and hatchets and hid on the island from his crew. Another source says he was paid with those items and did not want to go back when Mossel's ship departed in May or June 1613.

When Mossel arrived shortly after Christiaensen, he was not happy about the Rodriguez situation, who was now working as an interpreter and trader for Christiaensen. Rodriguez had established relationships with the local Native American tribes. When an opportunity arose, Mossel and his men decided they would beat Rodriguez but ultimately were rescued by Christiaensen's crew.

Block arrived as commander of the entire Van Tweenhuysen venture. Seeing the deadlock between the competitors for the trade, Block offered Mossel two-fifths of the trade and Christiaensen would get three-fifths. Block had his own idea about finding new fur trading opportunities as he had already been to the New World three times previously. That agreement did not last long. Mossel decided to go though the Hellgat (East River) but that was also Block's plan and therefore no agreements were reached as they headed off into the winter. Documents also state that some crewmembers from Christiaensen's ship were not content that Block had

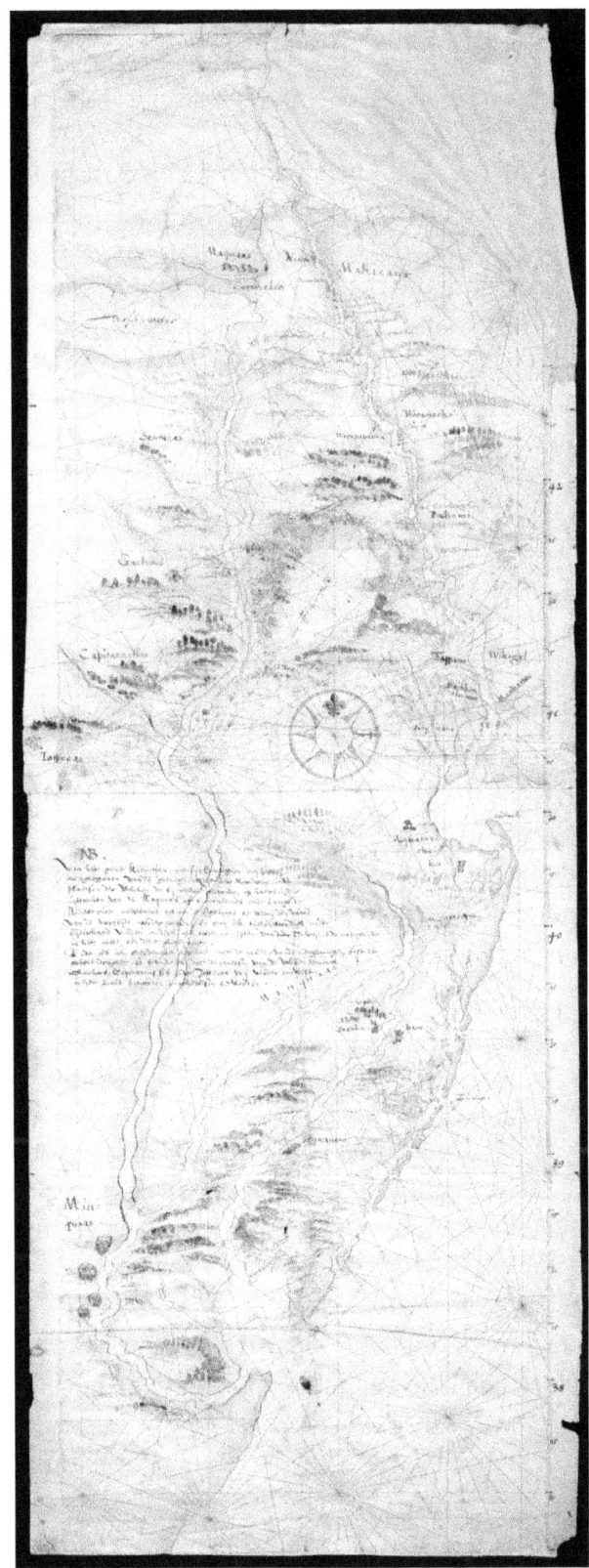

Cornelis Hendrickson created this map in 1616 after he explored the Delaware Bay and the lands between 38 and 40 degrees latitude with The *Onrust*.

struck a deal with Mossel.

Block and the *Tijger* were scheduled to leave in January 1614 but were delayed due to ice and a long winter. Then tragedy struck. In late January or early February 1614, the *Tijger* caught on fire. Was it accidental or arson? While other historians have written that the fire was an accident, this author believes it was arson and a possible explanation follows. The affidavits of Block and others do not discuss this in any detail.

The burning of the *Tijger* was likely arson. Once the mutineers decided to mutiny they knew that if they could get rid of one ship - the *Tijger* with its cannons- they would have a better and equal chance of battling it out with the *Fortuyn*, safer to have one boat chasing you than two. In addition, Block had six large cannons on board the *Tijger* and the mutineers did not want to tangle with those. One can assume there were several discussions about a mutiny when Block reduced the crew's profits as soon as they landed in New York Bay. The discussion about a mutiny would have been not only among Block's men but perhaps the *Fortuyn* sailors as well since four of them joined the mutiny that day. We can assume they were not happy about Block decreasing their profits in order to appease Mossel earlier. The majority of the mutineers were from Block's *Tijger*.

In addition, after the fire, Mossel offered to take in Block's crew and a larger share of the profits but Block ordered his crew not to go aboard. Half of Block's crew then mutinied, and along with members of the other ships, overtook the *Nachtegael*. Actually, the original plan was that the eight mutineers from Block's ship plotted to kill the crew on board the *Nachtegael*. After learning that Mossel and crew were going to go onshore the next day to collect firewood, they changed the plan to kill them and to just take the ship since there would be few people on board.

On March 6th 1614, Mossel's Supercargo took two sloops and 17 men up to the East River to trade under the objection of Block.

Once Mossel's ship was overtaken on March 7th, two more of Block's crew joined the pirates, four from the *Fortuyn* and two from Mossel's own crew joined the mutiny, 16 in total, plus a boy from Mossel's ship who most likely was forced to stay. They quickly threw out ballast, lifted the boat from the ground and placed it in the water, and then prepared their naval guns ready to fire and opened the portholes. Eight days later, Mossel's men, 17 of them plus the Supercargo, came back from a trade expedition and discovered that their ship was taken.

Mossel alerted Block and they went to the ship whereby Block tried to talk his crew into returning Mossel's ship. Block promised the mutineers that if they returned the ship, he would pretend nothing had happened, would give them full pay and put them ashore on land of their choice or dropped in another country. When the mutineers decided not to budge, Block and Mossel went to the *Onrust*, probably under construction nearby. They asked the crew there and some crewmembers of Mossel's to gather all their muskets, load them, along with spears and go to the heights, or mountains, near the ship and "hurt the rascals."[27]

Block's crew was not willing to go and asked Block who would take care of them if they got hurt. [27] Block replied that they would be taken care of and added to his crew, and after some hesitation, Mossel agreed to do the same. Under the direction of Thijs Mossel and Jan Kindt, Block's Supercargo, they went to the top of the mounts and fired on the mutineers all morning long, who in turn responded with their guns. The question of which mounts they shot from puzzles historians who have been trying to figure out exactly where the *Onrust* was built.

It may be that the *Onrust* was built somewhere near Governor's Island to protect the ship from the cold westerly winds during wintertime. It also seems that most of the activity, the mutiny and fight, occurred somewhere between the Hell Gat and the entrance of the East River, just north of Governors Island.

At noon, Mossel and Kindt came down from the mountain or high point and asked Block to take the *Onrust* to Christiaensen's ship and get help. Block sent Mossel and Kindt and three men to get the *Onrust*. As that occurred, Block and some crew members plus Mossel's crew descended near the mutineers and began shooting at them with their muskets. The mutineers returned fire and yelled to Block to stop firing or that night they would sneak up and burn the *Onrust*. That threat to burn the *Onrust* may be an indication that Block knew his men had intentionally burned the *Tijger* and were threatening to do it again. Perhaps Block never mentioned this in his

---

[27]Hart, Notarial Records, p. 88.

affidavit, as he believed if he were held accountable for the mutiny he would be responsible for the cost of losing the ship.

Apparently, all were poor marksmen as there is no indication that anyone was killed or injured during all the shooting back and forth.

On the 8th of March, the *Fortuyn* floated down the river barely missing the floating icebergs and picked up Block and company (minus 3 people who stayed with the *Onrust*). They then followed the retreating Nightingale to the mouth of the river. The remaining crew of Block and Mossel, however, refused to fight anymore even with Block promising them help if they got wounded. Instead, Block wrote a letter on his side's behalf that was sent to the mutineers and they responded, but there is no copy of that response believed to have survived or been found yet.

We also know that two of Block's crew, Hermen Hillbrantsen and Lolle Reijners, did not take part in the fight as they were "doing carpentry work" on the *Onrust*.[28]

Remarkably, the mutinous crew of the Nightingale sent ashore axes, kettles, and beads for Mossel and his crew and assumed their personal items as well which were stored in the *Fortuyn*. Mossel and crew used those items to trade with the Natives.

Block and his crew told their version of the story in an affidavit on July 24, 1614 and it is here we learn which crewmembers stayed with Block and did not take part in the mutiny.

They were:

Captain Adriaen Block from Amsterdam, Netherlands and is located in the province of North Holland. He was about 47.

Jan Kindt, [also spelled Kin or Kint]. Supercargo. Home base unknown. He was about 28 years old. He was the nephew of one of the partners of the van Tweenhuysen Company, Francoys Pelgrom and owners of the *Tijger* and *Fortuyn*.

Jacob de Vries, Mate. From Franeker which is a city in Friesland. He was about 40.

Hendrick Scholthouwer, Surgeon. From Montfort which is a town in the province of Limburg. He was about 25.

Hans Romboutsen, Boatswain. A boatswain is a deck foreman. From Antwerp which is a city in present Belgium, but then southern Netherlands in the province of Flanders. He was about 27.

Anthony Janssen, Constable. From Amsterdam. He was about 30.

Hermen Hillebrantsen, Carpenter. From Amsterdam in the province of North Holland. He was about 23 and probably the master shipwright who built the *Onrust*.

---

[28] Hart, Prehistory, p. 90.

Vincent Janss, Cook. From Monnikendam which is a city in the province of North Holland. He was about 29.

Lolle Reijners. It appears he was a carpenter. From Bolsward which is in the province of Friesland, the Netherlands. He was about 24.

Claes Woutersen. From Medemblik which is in the province of North Holland and region of West Frisia (West Friesland), age about 25. He was one of the mutineers on the *Nightingale* but declared that he was taken prisoner and not a mutineer. It is not clear what ship he was from.

Cornelis Hendrickson. From Monnikendam. Appointed Skipper of the Onrust after Block went back home on the Fortune.

We also know the names of some of Christiaensen's crew who did not mutiny:

Hendrick Christiaensen from Amsterdam, Skipper. Age unknown.

Frans Jansen, Cook. From Monnikendam, which is a city in the province of North Holland. He was about 26 years old.

Gerbrant Jansen, Chief Boatswain. From Kolhorn, a town in the province of North Holland. He was about 34.

Esger Annes, Constable. From Hindeloopen, a city in the north of the Netherlands on Lake IJsselmeer. He was about 30.

Jochem Jochemsen. From Danzig, a cosmopolitan city on the Baltic Sea which is now part of Poland. He was about 25.

Pieter Pietersen, Boatswain. From Amsterdam. He was about 25.

Jacop [Jacob?] Eelkens, Supercargo. Address unknown. He was about 21.

Jacop [Jacob?] Floressen, Boatswain. From Medemblik, a town in North Holland. He was about 23.

Dirck Clasen, Boatswain. From Alkamaar, a city in North Holland. He was about 28.

Jacob Servaes, Cooper. From Vrede. He was about 23.

We also know some of the names of Mossel's crew from the affidavits:

Thijs Volckertsz Mossel, Skipper. From Monnikendam. He was about 41.

Hans Jorissen, Supercargo. Homeport unknown. Age unknown.

Jan Gerritss, Boatswain. From Rotterdam, a port city in the province of South Holland. He was about 40.

Dirck Andriess, Smith. From Dithmarschen, a district in Schleswig-Holstein, Germany. He was about 26.

We also know from the records that Mathijs Hartoch from Rotterdam, one of Mossel's crew, became a pirate and was one of the mutineers that stole the *Nachtegael*.

If ten of Block's crew mutinied as described in the documents, then nine did not, which would indicate that the original *Tijger's* crew was 19 men plus Block. There may also have been some boys with the ship. It is unclear if Woutersen was a Block crewmember or member from one of the other ships. If he was a part of Block's crew, then the total would be twenty-one members for the *Tijger*.

The mutineers took the *Nachtegael* to the West Indies but came back to the Hudson River several months later to clean the ship and make repairs. Block and company had found a way back home by then. The mutineers then set sail for Newfoundland (Terra Nova), but did not find it so they headed to Spain. They ended up in Ireland. Ireland was becoming a popular location for pirates at the time. In fact, the Spaniards took over the Barbary Coast by 1614 and 28 pirate ships then decided to move their operations to Ireland.

"Mutineer" Claes Woutersen from Medemblik returned to the Netherlands claiming he was taken prisoner and not a mutineer. He defended Block's version of the story-- that Block had nothing to do with the mutiny. Mossel's owners accused Block as being part of the mutiny. This might infer that Woutersen was a Block crewmember originally. Nothing further is known of the mutineers.[29]

When the Tijger burned, Block had no choice but to build a ship. It was either freeze to death in the middle of winter or build the *Onrust,* the Dutch word for *"restless"* and certainly an appropriate name considering the situation they faced.

In the 17th century up to modern times, boat owners customarily pulled their ship onshore and out of the water as far as possible. If that was the case here, would Block's ship not have burned completely if they could not have pushed it back in the water when it was on fire? While it is not written it likely that while the *Tijger* was on fire the crew went aboard throwing everything overboard: ropes, sails, tools, and especially the shipwright tools, plus 23-year-old Herman Hillebrantsen, the shipwright who did not join the mutiny. It is likely that Hillebrantsen supervised the construction of the *Onrust* along with another carpenter, Lolle Reijner. What is remarkable is that in order to build a ship, a number of very specialized artisans besides the shipwright (probably Hillebrantsen) are also needed. Artisans needed are a blacksmith, block maker, sail maker, rope maker, sculptor (for figurehead and other ornaments), glazier, lantern maker, coppersmith, flag maker, compass maker, and caulkers and driller for making treenails. Some of these items must have been rescued or recovered from the burnt *Tijger,* or borrowed from the *Fortuyn*. Conjecture is that some of the crew from the *Fortuyn* also helped in constructing the *Onrust*. After all, Block was captain of both the *Tijger* and *Fortuyn* so he was technically in control of both crews. As another thought, could the *Onrust* actually have been a rebuild of the leftover unburned hull remains of the *Tijger*. If the *Tijger* only burned to the water line, a rebuilt boat could explain why the newly christened *Onrust* was float worthy only four

---

[29]Simon Hart,. 1959. "Declaration of one of the capturers of the ship the "Nachtegael." Pages 97-98. The Prehistory of the New Netherland Company. Amsterdam Notarial Records of the first Dutch voyages to the Hudson. City Archives of Amsterdam. City of Amsterdam Press, 1959. 105 pp.

months after the fire on the *Tijger*?

We know the *Onrust* was float worthy by March because on March 4th, 1614, Block took the *Onrust* to Mossel's ship; Christiaensen had sailed up the river the day before to trade. So if the *Tijger* burned in late January or early February and he was moving the *Onrust* on March 4th, that was a remarkably short time to build the *Onrust* unless they had salvaged a great deal of material from the burned out *Tijger*. On the other hand, being trapped thousands of miles from home on an island in the dead of winter is a good incentive to work hard and fast.

Some writers have indicated that the *Onrust* may have been built in Albany but there is not enough evidence to support it, especially considering the timeline of events. We know that it takes three days for the boats today to get from New York Bay to Albany under diesel power, so it is highly unlikely that the *Onrust* would have been able to go from Albany to New York Bay under the circumstances described in the Block affidavits in such short time periods - and in the middle of winter.

We do know the size of the original *Onrust* was 38 feet over the keel, 44 1/2 feet long and 11 1/2 feet wide and weighed 8 *last* (16 tons). A *last* is equal to two tons. No documentary evidence exists that Block built huts on the island and was fed by the local Native population as some historians claim. However, there might be some truth to that statement since Rodriguez who was now working for Christiaensen and Block had been living on the island for a year. All three men, Block, Christiaensen and Rodriquez made relationships with the Native Americans, the first two on previous visits, and could have persuaded them to help the stranded crew.

Our knowledge of the mutiny and events that followed are available as affidavits in the archives in Amsterdam, in Hart's *Prehistory* book and Stokes' *Iconography*. Several of Block's and Mossel's crews swore out affidavits telling their version of the story. Obviously, both were slanted toward their version of the truth and we may never know the whole story.

The *Fortuyn*, under Block's orders, finally sailed up the Hudson and the crew built a fur-trading fort on the tip of Castle Island, now present day Port of Albany, called Fort Nassau. There is a record that the *Onrust* visited Fort Nassau in 1614, probably to check on the success of the fort construction. There may have been several versions of Fort Nassau as reports of the fort being flooded out forced the relocating onto the mainland and the building of Fort Orange in 1624.

Fortunately for the stranded crew and the fact that Christiansen's *Fortuyn* was too small to bring everyone back, two ships - the *Vos* and a second *Fortuyn* - entered the bay. The *Vos* was from Amsterdam while the second *Fortuyn* was from Hoorn. Block had to agree to give the newcomers an equal share in the trade for bringing the crew and furs back. Each company agreed to take one quarter of the total, and that was a loss to Block. Block and his Supercargo Jan Kindt had purchased them all in the first place.

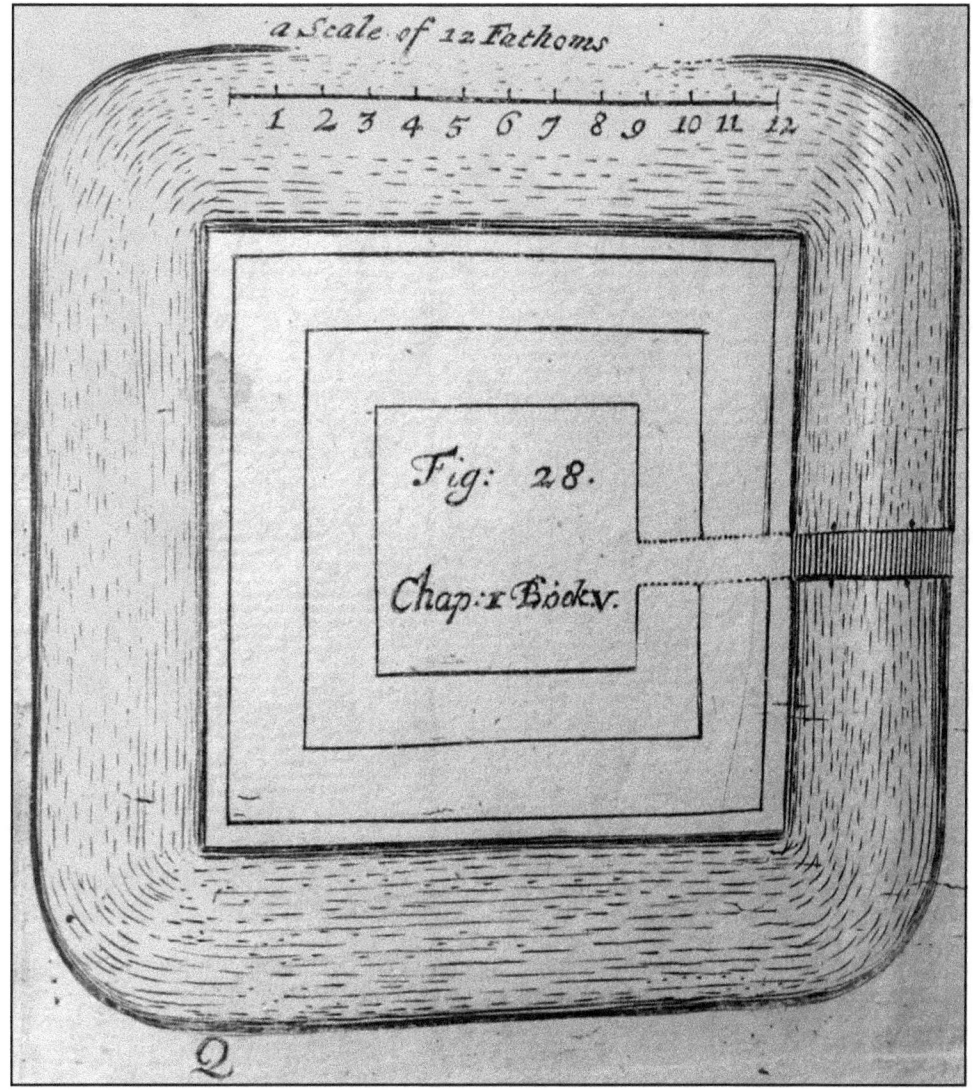

Planimetric view of what Fort Nassau may have looked like. This drawing of a "redoubt" appeared in the book "The New Method of Fortification, as practiced by Monsieur de Vauban," published in 1693 and has the same dimensions and layout as Fort Nassau.

Before he went back to Amsterdam, Block took the *Onrust* and explored the New York coastal areas and rivers, sailed through the treacherous passage called Helgat (Hell Gate) in the East River (again, probably for the third time), explored the harbors of Long Island and Connecticut discovering the Housatonic and Thames Rivers, and sailed up the Connecticut (deVersche River) River past the site of Hartford. The *Onrust* continued on to Narragansett and Buzzards Bays, and finally Cape Cod when Block gave the command to Cornelis Hendrickson.

In June 1614, the *Fortuyn* One and Two and *Vos* left for the Netherlands reaching their destination on July 22nd, or 23rd. On the way, Christensen's *Fortuyn* picked up Block near Cape Cod. Block gave the *Onrust* to Cornelis Hendrickson (c. 1572-1650) who took the ship south into Godins Bay (Delaware Bay) and up the Zuyd Rivier (South River) to the Schuylkill River

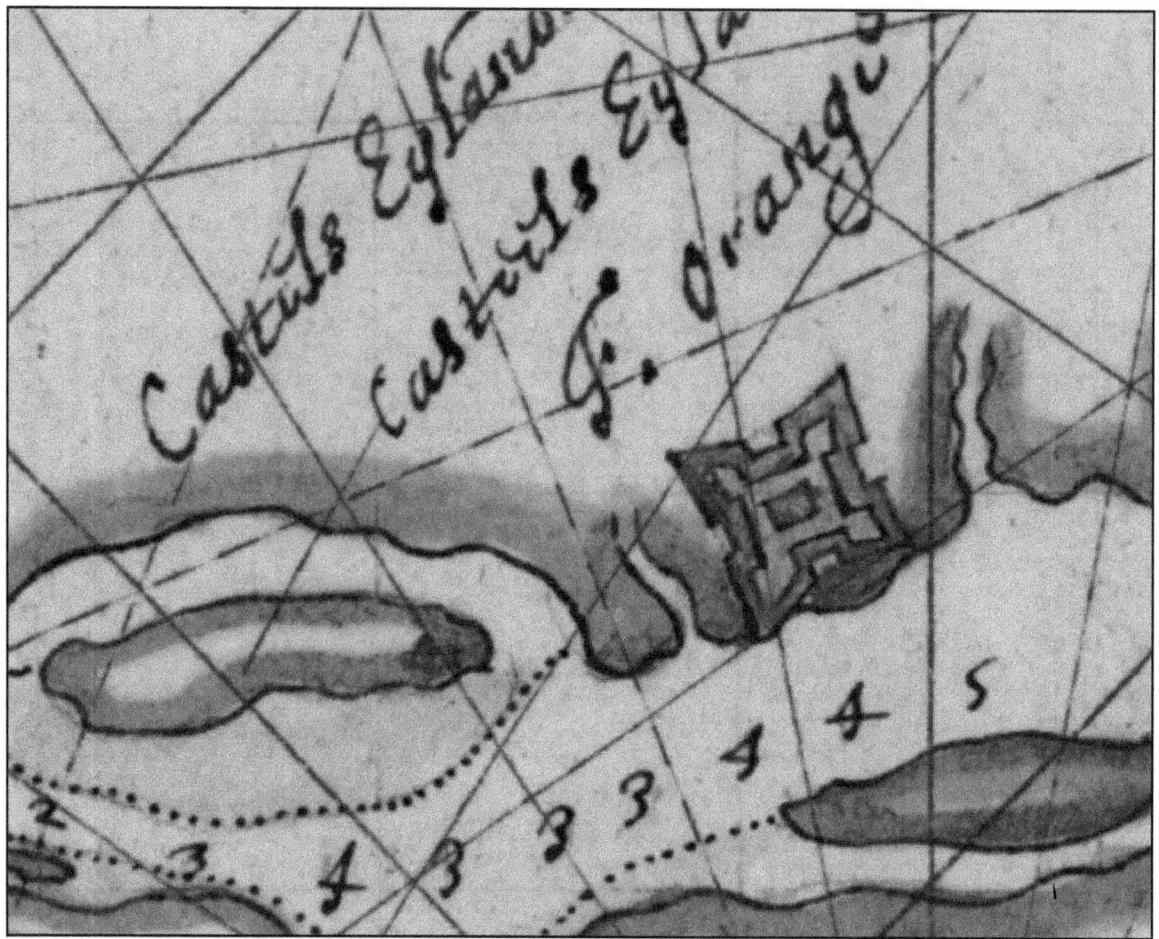

Fort Nassau at the north tip of Castle Island and Fort Orange to the right on the mainland is shown on this c.1639 (or earlier) map attributed to Joan Vinceboons. Source: Library of Congress.

until 1616.

Both Block and Hendrickson prepared maps so that van Tweenhuysen could seek exclusive rights for trading based on their voyages of all the land between 38 and 45 degrees North Latitude. These were the first two accurate maps of the Northeastern coast and much of the interior. These explorers were also the first to locate all of the known Native American villages.

Block's map was the first to have printed the name New Netherland (Niew Nederlandt). Hendrickson went to the Delaware Bay. He reached the south boundary of Maryland where it touches the Atlantic and the latitude of present day Philadelphia so, in fact, he explored the Delaware Bay and River, along with the Christiana Creek and Schuylkill which included all the territory between the 38th and 40th parallels. While exploring the Christiana Creek, he came upon a group of Natives and traded with them. He also paid a ransom for three Dutchmen who were captured earlier. He also produced a map.

Captain Cornelis Hendrickson was born in 1572 in Utrecht, Holland, Netherlands, and was the

Adriaen Block's neighborhood as it exists today showing his house and the Montelbaanstoren on the Oudeschans still standing. Photo by Marieke Leeverink.

Block's neighborhood (and house) as it appeared in c. 1616-18 thanks to this "Profile of Amsterdam" etching, by Pieter van der Keere. The Montelbaen Tower is to the left. Source Wikipedia.

son of Lambert Hendrickson. He married Sonnetje Rutger and had a son, Daniel, born March 4, 1650 in Utrecht. As a result of his voyages he was the first European to set foot on the soil of Pennsylvania and West Jersey. He was the discoverer of the Raritan and Schuylkill Rivers, and explored the Delaware River to and area of a falls at the present site of Trenton. He also navigated Barnegat Inlet and the Toms River onboard the *Onrust*, becoming the first European explorer to set foot on what became Ocean County in New Jersey. He died in 1650.

The States General of the Netherlands issued a proclamation on March 27, 1614 that anyone discovering new countries, harbors and passageways would have an exclusive patent that was good for four voyages over a period of three years. On October 11, 1614, such a patent was issued that declared all the territory between the 40th and 45th parallels, known as New Netherland, would be in the control of a new company called the New Netherland Company. The patent began on January 1, 1615. This was the result of the voyages of Adrian Block. The New Netherland Company was actually comprised of the Van Tweenhuysen Company that Block worked for, the Hans Claesz Company, Gerrit Witsen's company and one from the city of Hoorn, which was an interesting combination since all of them were in competition with each other. The principals were:

Gerrit Jacob Witsen, Jonas Cornelisz. Witsen. Simon Wiilemsz. Nooms (the owners of the *Vosje*);

Hans Hunger, Paulus Pelgrom, Lambert van Tweenhuysen (owners of the *Tijger* which burned and the *Fortuyn*);

Arnout van Liebergen, Wessel Schenck, Hans Claesz. and Barent Sweers (owners of the *Nachtegael,* taken and turned into a pirate ship), all merchants from the city of Amsterdam;

Pieter Clementsz. Brouwer, Jan Clementsz. Kies and Cornelis Volckertsz. [or Volkertsz?] (owners of the second *Fortuyn*) and all merchants from the city of Hoorn.

While Jonas Witsen (at the time, Councilor) and Gerrit Jacob Witsen (Former Burgomaster of Amsterdam) were mentioned first in the patent and the ship *Vosje* went out on the voyage, not much is known about their disposition in this arrangement.

Even before the ink had dried on the New Netherland Company patent, they had to go after a competitor the 'Amsterdam Company' under the leadership of Albert Geritsz. Ruyl who fitted up the *Fortuyn*. He argued that he had been the first, or at least second, to explore those waters and did not know why he was excluded from the patent. On October 24, 1614, the directors of New Netherland Company offered to take over the ship. Some form of agreement was struck though nothing on paper has been found.

The New Netherland Patent ran out on January 1, 1618. They tried to get a new patent that included the 38th to 40th parallels but no avail. They asked for an extension of the old one but that was not granted either. Fate was sealed when Hendrick Eelckern and Adriaen Jansz. from the company at Amsterdam requested the States General and Prince Maurice permission to carry on trade in New Netherland on October 9th, 1618, and the patent was granted. Hendrick Christiaensen took the *Swarte Beer* to the Hudson at the same time, although he was given notice not to interfere with the trading of the other company.

It was Christiaensen's last voyage. In the spring of 1619, a group of Natives came aboard the ship near Governor's Island or Manhattan, presumably to trade, and killed him and a large part of the crew before they were driven way by two shots from their guns. Only five of the crew survived and were badly injured. Hendrick Christiaensen, perhaps the first to begin trading with the Natives, was to be no more at the hands of the very people that made him rich. Wassenaer blames one of the Native boys that he and Block brought to the Netherlands.

"'This Orson was a thoroughly wicked fellow, and after his return to his own country was the cause of Hendrick Christiaensen's death. But he was paid in like coin; he got a bullet as his recompense."[30]

The New Netherland Company continued until 1623 and was often just called the Lambert van Tweenhuysen and Company. His interest in the region disappeared as the *Geoctroyeerde Westindische Compagnie* or Dutch West India Company (known as the GWC) later took over. With the GWC charter issued in 1621, private trade in New Netherland ended for the most part. With the building of forts in Albany and Manhattan by the GWC, the amount of furs shipped back to the Netherlands increased. During the beginning of the company's operations from 1624-1627, some 26,458 furs were so shipped. Ironically, today you can see the West India Company office building built in 1642 from Adriaen Block's house that is also still standing. What ultimately happened to the *Onrust* is not completely known. Hendrickson left the ship behind for future trading to take upriver for trade by future New Netherland Company voyages due to its small size and could easily navigate the smaller rivers and streams. A common practice was to leave boats, as evidenced later when the company of Hendrick Eelkens and Hans Jorisz Honton tried to get paid for what they left behind - two yachts, a sloop, Zaandam barge and Biscayan sloop. On September 11, 1626, Eelkens and Honton sought to be reimbursed from the Dutch West India Company that confiscated the boats. One of those yachts was 16 tons, the same size as the *Onrust*. There has been some research by a Dutch historian that indicates the *Onrust* may have been renamed and used by employees of the New Netherland Company in later years, exploring the Delaware and that perhaps sailed over the Atlantic to the Netherlands.

Adriaen Block never went back to North America, nor did he ever work for the New Netherlands Company in which he help founded. Christiaensen, on the other hand, made five or more voyages after Block quit before he was killed by Native Americans.

---

[30] Nicolaes Van Waasenaer,. "Historicsch Verhael" in Narratives of New Netherland: 1609-1664. John Franklin Jameson. 1909. Applewood's American Philosophy and Religion Series. P. 81.

Second page of the *Grant of Exclusive Trade to New Netherland by the States-General of the United Netherlands; October 11, 1614 mentioning New Netherland for the first time.* Courtesy Marieke Leeverink.

The troubles Block encountered on the last voyage was more than likely the end of the rope for him. At 47 years of age, he may have decided it was better to work closer to home. In 1615, he was general director of the entire Northern Company's whaling operations in Spitsbergen, Norway. Since van Tweenhuysen was a director of the Northern Company, he may have landed Block the job for his earlier service to his company.

On March 21, 1626, Block sold his ship *Drie Coningen* ("Three Queens") which weighed 60 lasts (about 120 tons), and "last sailed by himself" to skipper Reijer Vredericxss of Vlieland. Block continued to live in his house in Amsterdam and died the next year on April 7, 1627. He is buried next to his wife who predeceased him in 1625. Both are buried in the *Oude Kerk* ("old church"), which is Amsterdam's oldest parish church, consecrated in 1306. However, Block's plot is unmarked and therefore unknown where he is actually buried. Incidentally, buried in the same cemetery is diamond merchant Killian Van Rensselaer. Van Rensselaer would take Block's new explored territory of New Netherland in a new direction shortly after Block's death. In 1630, Van Rensselaer developed one of the first successful Dutch colonies in New Netherland called Rensselaerwyck in the upper Hudson Mohawk Valley, near the fort that Block ordered built. It is the present Capital Region.[31]

The adventures of Adriaen Block and the *Onrust* laid the groundwork for the European colonization for current day New York and five other states: Delaware, Pennsylvania, Maryland, Connecticut, and New Jersey. Block and his people produced the first two accurate maps of the Northeast coast and interiors of the land, plus accurately located all the known Native tribes in the region. In today's vernacular, the *Onrust* was the first "green" construction project that can boast "Made in New York."

New Netherland grew into a rich and culturally diverse and politically robust set of self governed communities. Dutch respect for freedom of conscience and choice and the ability for women to enjoy legal, civil, and economic rights unknown by their British counterparts in America was the genesis of what we all enjoy today as the American way of life.

Grant of Exclusive Trade to New Netherland
by the States-General of the United Netherlands; October 11, 1614

The States-General of the United Netherlands, to all to whom these presents shall come, greeting.

Whereas Gerrit Jacobz Witssen, ancient Burgomaster of the city Amsterdam, Jonas Witssen, Simon Morrissen, owners of the ship named the Little Fox, whereof Jan de With has been skipper; Jans Hongers, Paulus Pelgrom, Lambrecht van Tweenhuyzen, owners of the two ships named the Tiger and the Fortune, whereof Adriaen Block and Henrick Corstiaenssen were skippers; Arnolt van Lybergen, Wessel Schenck, Hans Claessen, and Berent Sweertssen, owners of the ship named the Nightingale, whereof Thys Volckertssen was skipper, merchants of the aforesaid city Amsterdam, and Pieter Clementssen Bronwer,

---

[31]Jaap Jacobs. Dutch Proprietary Manors in America: The Patroonships in New Netherland. Chapter ten. In, Roper, L. H., & Ruymbeke, B. V. (2007). Constructing Early Modern empires: Proprietary ventures in the Atlantic world, 1500-1750. Leiden: Brill. pp. 301-326.

Jan Clementssen Kies, and Cornelis Volckertssen, merchants of the city of Hoorn, owners of the ship named the Fortuyn, whereof Cornelis Jacobssen May was skipper, all now associated in one company, have respectfully represented to us that they, the petitioners, after great expenses and damages by loss of ships and other dangers, had, during the present year, discovered and found with the above named five ships certain new lands situate in America between New France and Virginia, the sea coast whereof lie between forty and forty-five degrees of latitude, and now called New Netherland. And whereas we did, in the month of March last, for the promotion and increase of commerce, cause to be published a certain general consent and charter setting forth that whosoever should thereafter discover new havens, lands, places, or passages might frequent or cause to be frequented, for four voyages, such newly discovered and found places, passages, havens, or lands to the exclusion of all others from visiting or frequenting the same from the United Netherlands until the said first discoverers and finders shall themselves have completed the said four voyages or cause the same to be done within the time prescribed for that purpose, under the penalties expressed in the said octroy, etc.; they request that we would accord to them due act of the aforesaid octroy in the usual form.

Which, being considered, we, therefore, in our Assembly, having heard the pertinent report of the petitioners relative to the discoveries and finding of the said new countries between the above named limits and degrees and also of their adventures, have consented and granted, and by these presents do consent and grant, to the said petitioners now united into one company that they shall be privileged exclusively to frequent or cause to be visited the above newly discovered lands, situate in America between New France and Virginia, whereof the sea coasts lie between the fortieth and forty-fifth degrees of latitude, now named New Netherland, as can be seen by a figurative map hereunto annexed, and that for four voyages within the term of three years, commencing the first of January, sixteen hundred and fifteen next ensuing, or sooner, without it being permitted to any other person from the United Netherlands, to sail to, navigate, or frequent the said newly discovered lands, havens, or places, either directly or indirectly within the said three years, on pain of confiscation of the vessel and cargo wherewith infraction hereof shall be attempted, and a fine of fifty thousand Netherland ducats for the benefit of said discoverers or finders; provided, nevertheless, that by these presents we do not intend to prejudice or diminish any of our former grants or charters. And it is also our intention that if any disputes or differences arise from these our concessions, they shall be decided by ourselves.

We, therefore, expressly command all governors, justices, officers, magistrates, and inhabitants of the aforesaid united countries that they allow the said company peaceably and quietly to enjoy the whole benefit of this our grant and consent, ceasing all contradictions and obstacles to the contrary. For such we have found to appertain to the public service. Given under our seal, paraple, and signature of our Secretary at the Hague the 11th of October, 1614.

Block's Timeline

Based on the archival records in Amsterdam, Dutch Captain Adriaen Block made four voyages to the New world between 1611 and 1614 in which he mapped out the Northeastern Coast and Interior in great detail. The famous 1614 *Block Map* showed for the first time the locations of all known Native American villages. His solid relations with the Natives not only enabled him to draw a detailed map of their living areas but also allowed him to build a ship on their shores and a fort on their land. By 1614, six years before the Pilgrims arrived, Block built the *Onrust* on the shores of New York Bay and had already made agreements and received permission from the Natives to build Fort Nassau near modern Albany. His extensive relations enabled him to lay the framework that resulted in the founding of New Netherland.

Block's Voyages to New Netherland

1609
Henry Hudson returns to the Dutch Republic after an unsuccessful attempt to find the Northwest Passage but alerting the Dutch citizenry about trading possibilities with the local inhabitants.

1611.
As Supercargo for Cornelis Rijser aboard the ship *St. Pieter*, Block makes his first trading voyage in the New World.

1612 February
Block purchases the 110 ton *Fortuyn* for the Van Tweenhuysen Company of Amsterdam to undertake his second trip and set up successful trade with the Native population.

1612 Fall
Again with the *Fortuyn*, Block undertakes a third trading voyage to the Hudson River area, explores more of the area and collects additional information for his future map. Among his crew are Hendrick Christiaensen and Jacob Eelkins.

1613 Fall
As Captain of The *Tyger*, Block makes his fourth and final voyage to the Hudson along with Hendrick Christiaensen who now captains the *Fortuyn*. The *Tyger* burns in New York Bay.

1613/1614 Winter
Block and his crew build The *Onrust*, the first yacht and fur trading vessel built in the New World, launched in April 1614. On Block's orders, Hendrick Christiaensen sails up the Hudson and with the permission of local Native inhabitants builds Fort Nassau. The *Onrust* soon follows and visits Fort Nassau.

1616-1618
As a result of Block's voyages and maps, the States General grants the newly formed New Netherland Company a three year exclusive trade agreement with the Indigenous Peoples of all the land from 40 to 45 degrees north latitude.

1621
West India Company (WIC) forms and takes control of former New Netherland Company region.

1624-1625
Fort Orange (Albany) established in upper Hudson River in 1624; New Amsterdam (NYC) formed at the mouth of river in 1625, both by WIC.

1630
Rensselaerswyk (Upper Hudson), Pavonia (Jersey City) and Swaenedael (Lewes, Delaware) are established and Dutch settlements begin.

Bibliography

Anderson, R. C. (1955). Seventeenth-century rigging; a handbook for model-makers. London: P. Marshall. 146 pp.

Barbour, Violet. "Dutch and English Merchant Shipping in the Seventeenth Century." The Economic History Review, 1930. A2. No. 2:261-290.

Cawston, George and Keane, Augustus Henry. 1896. The Early Chartered Companies (A.D. 1296-1858), Pg. 43.

Cawston, G., & Keane, A. H. (2004). The early chartered companies: (A.D. 1296-1858). Honolulu, HI: University Press of the Pacific. pp. 216-230.

Anderson, A. (1787). An historical and chronological deduction of the origin of commerce, from the earliest accounts: Containing an history of the great commercial interests ...; in 4 volumes. London: Robson, Payne.

De Winter W.; Burningham, N. "Distinguishing different types of early 17th-century Dutch Jacht and ship through multivariate morphometric analysis of contemporary maritime art." International Journal of Nautical Archaeology 30. Nov. 2001. No. 1:57-73.

Duhamel du Monceau, M. Grondbeginselen van den scheepsbouw, of Werkdadige verhandeling der scheepstimmerkunst. Amsterdam:InsGravvenhaage: By Ottho van Thol, Boekverkopers., 1759. 428 pp.

Gebhard Johan Fredrik. Het leven van Mr. Nicolaas Cornelisz. Witsen. (1641-1717). J.W. Leeflang, 1881. 1054 pp.

Harjo, S. S. (n.d.). Nation to nation: Treaties between the United States & American Indian Nations. 272 pps.

Hart, Simon. The Prehistory of the New Netherland Company. Amsterdam Notarial Records of the First Dutch Voyages on the Hudson. City of Amsterdam Press, 1959. 105 pp.

Hasslof, Olof. "Carvel Construction Technique Nature and Origin. Folk-Living. 1958. 21-22: 49-60.

Hoving, A. J., Wildeman, D., & Witsen, N. (2012). Nicolaes Witsen and shipbuilding in the Dutch Golden Age. College Station: Texas A & M University Press. 310 pp.

Hoving, A. J. "A 17th Century Dutch 134- Foot Pinas: A Reconstruction after Aeloude en Hedendaegse Scheepsbouwen Bestier by Nicolaes Witsen 1671." Pts. 1 and 2. . International Journal for Nautical Archaeology 17,1988. No. 3: 211–22; No. 4: 331–38.

Jacobs Jaap. Dutch Proprietary Manors in America: The Patroonships in New Netherland. In Constructing Early Modern Empires. Proprietary Ventures in the Atlantic World, 1500-1750, Ed. by L.H. Roper and B. Van Ruymbeke Brill, 2007. Pp, 301-326.

Kalm, P. (1972). Travels into North America. Barre, MA: Imprint Society. Pp 37-40

Kaye, P. L. (n.d.). English colonial administration under Lord Clarendon, 1660-1667. 159 pp.

Mainwaring, Sir Henry. c. 1625, Seaman's Dictionary. Ed. with notes by Mainwaring, G. E. & Perrin, W. G. London: Navy Records Society, 1920.

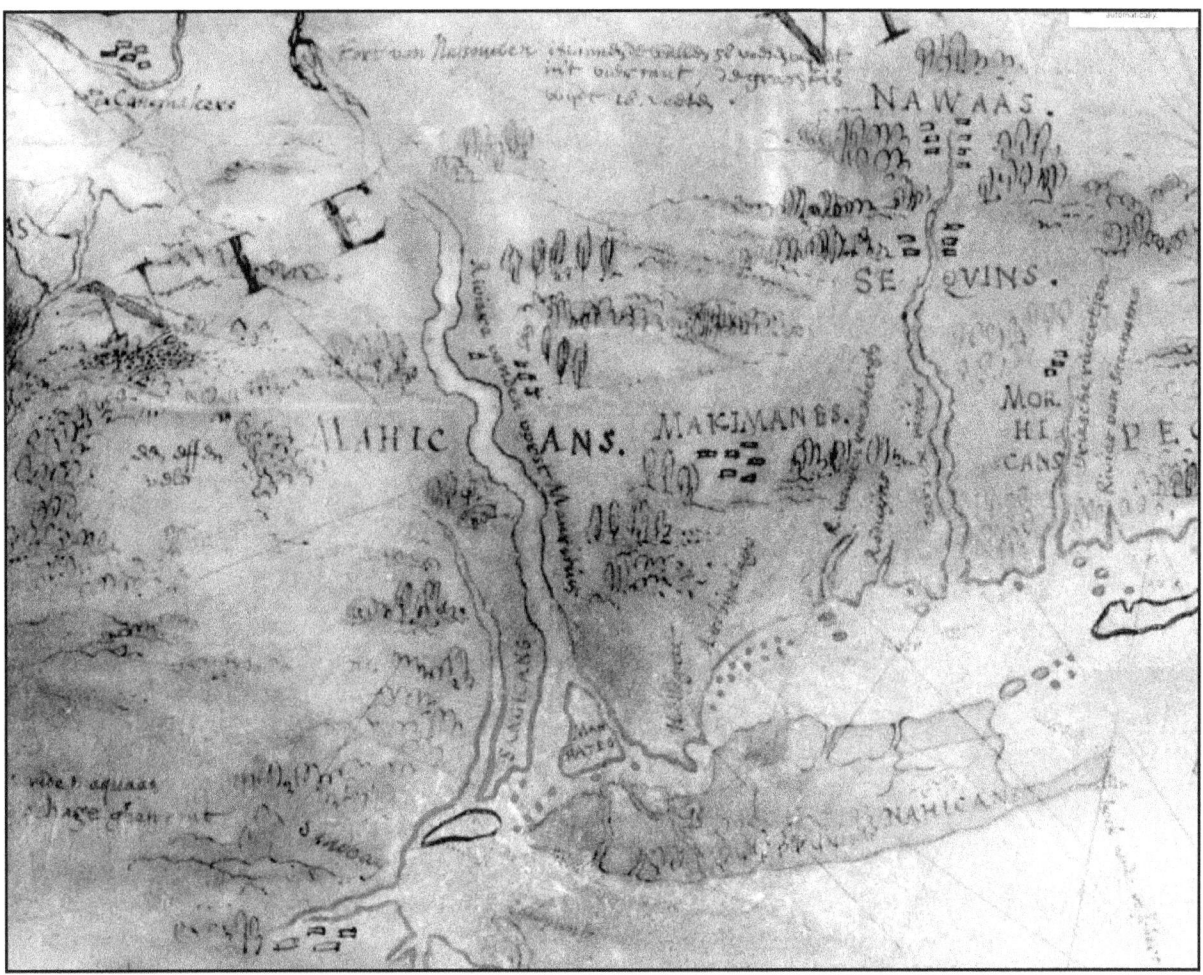

The Hudson Valley in New York State as it appeared on Block's 1614 map. The Hudson Valley became the center of Dutch settlements in North America. Fort Nassau appears on the top of this section of the map. Fort Nassau eventually became present day Albany, New York. The descriptor New Netherland appears for the first time on this map.

Mason, Herbert B., Ed. Encyclopaedia of Ships and Shipping. The Shipping Encyclopaedia Limited. London: Chichester House, 1908. 749 pp.

McBride, Peter W. J. "The Mary, Charles II's Yacht: Her History, Importance and Ordnance." International Journal of Nautical Archaeology, 2, 1973. No. 1:61-79

McBride, Peter W. J. "The Mary, Charles II's Yacht: The Discovery of the wreck." International Journal of Nautical Archaeology, 2, 1973. No 2.1:59-73.

McKee, E., 1976, "Identification of timbers from old ships of north-western European origin." IJNA, , 1976. No. 5: 3-12.

Milholland, Sharon Kay. Native Voices and Native Values in Sacred Landscapes Management: Bridging the Indigenous Values Gap on Public Lands Through Co-Management Policy. Dissertation. University of Arizona. 2008. 255 pps.

Reinder Reinders and Kees Paul, Eds.. "Carvel Construction Technique Skeleton-first, Shell-first. Fifth

International Symposium on Boat and Ship Archaeology, Amsterdam 1988." Oxbow Monograph 12. 1991. 194 pp.

Tossavainen, Jouko. 1994. "Dutch Forest Products Trade in the Baltic. Department of History and Ethnology. Master's Thesis. University of Jyvaskyla. 149 pp.

Van Waasenaer, Nicolaes. "Historicsch Verhael" in Narratives of New Netherland: 1609-1664. John Franklin Jameson. 1909. Applewood's American Philosophy and Religion Series. P. 78

Van Yk, Cornelis. De Nederlandse Scheeps- bouw-konst Open Gestelt. Amsterdam: Jan ten Hoorn, 1697.

Wagenaar, Jan. Amsterdam, in zyne opkomst, aanwas, geschiedenissen, voorregten, koophandel, gebouwen, kerkenstaat, schoolen, schutterye, gilden en regeeringe. In Dutch. Isaak Tirion, Publisher, 1768. 495 pp.

Witsen, Nicolaes. Aeloude en Hedendaegse Scheepsbouw en Bestier. . . . Amsterdam: Casparus Commelijn. Broer and Jan Appelaer, 1671.